Math, Literature and Unifix®
Making the Connection

by
Richard J. Callan
and
Don S. Balka

Educational Resources

Order Number 2-146
ISBN 1-58324-107-8

A B C D E F 03 02 01

Educational Resources
395 Main Street
Rowley, MA 01969
www.worldteacherspress.com

Contents

About the Authors

Don S. Balka, Ph.D., is a noted mathematics educator who has presented numerous workshops on the use of mathematics manipulatives with elementary, middle and high school students at national and regional conferences of the National Council of Teachers of Mathematics, at state conferences and at in-service training for school districts throughout the world. He is a former junior high and high school mathematics teacher, and is currently a Professor in the Mathematics Department at Saint Mary's College, Notre Dame, Indiana.

Richard J. Callan has been a public school teacher in Indiana for 25 years and holds his BS and MS from Indiana University. He conducts staff development workshops and makes presentations on children's literature, assessment and manipulatives. In 1995, he received the Presidential Award for Elementary School Mathematics and appears in *Who's Who in America*. He was a contributing author to the *Indiana Mathematics Proficiency Guide*s in 1991 and 1997.

Introduction

Incorporating children's literature into your mathematics instruction provides a new and rich environment for children to learn mathematics, to appreciate mathematics in diverse settings and to practice reading, communication and comprehension skills. The intent of the authors is to introduce teachers to the vast amount of children's literature that supports mathematics teaching. As students progress through the mathematics curriculum, a deliberate effort to include many math-related stories will provide a wealth of opportunities for explorations, investigations and inquiries into mathematics.

This book was written to help teachers teach mathematical topics in a non-threatening way through the use of children's literature and by integrating manipulatives as part of the work. Books that are presented in **Math, Literature and Unifix**® have been selected for their appropriateness for mathematics instruction according to core topics, many of which are contained in the National Council of Teachers of Mathematics **Standards 2000: Standards and Principles for School Mathematics**. Each book may be adapted for several different grade levels.

As you peruse the contents, note that for each book the following components are provided:

- ◆ Title, Author, Publisher, Date, ISBN Number
- ◆ Story Summary
- ◆ Grade Level
- ◆ Concepts or Skills
- ◆ Objectives
- ◆ Materials Needed
- ◆ Activities
- ◆ Writing Activities
- ◆ Reinforcement Ideas

A teacher may use any of the activities he or she deems appropriate for mathematics instruction. One of the more important aspects of this book is that teachers will be able to use the literature, not for just one topic, but with many topics to expand and extend mathematics learning. Teachers can use the stories and activities to develop their own thematic or mathematics units and teaching lessons. In that regard, the readability of a book should not be the determining factor as to whether or not it is used for instruction. Instead, the emphasis should be placed on motivating children to learn different mathematical topics, by using children's literature as a basis for learning.

A teacher may have other children's literature books that can be used in teaching a particular concept. Additional books relating similar concepts and skills are listed when appropriate.

As a springboard for assessment, writing activities have been presented for each book. Some are designed to provide feedback to the teacher as to whether or not students understand the mathematics, while others are designed for writing similar stories incorporating the concepts or skills. A teacher may have his or her own writing activities to use for particular books.

Didax Educational Resources

The reinforcement component for each book provides teachers with ideas for fortifying student understanding of the mathematics. Many of the ideas incorporate manipulatives in a performance setting, whereas other ideas come out of writing assignments or paper-pencil tasks.

Bookmarks for children to use with their own reading books or library books are included at the end of the book. Each bookmark lists books for a particular mathematics topic. These may be duplicated on colored card stock or regular paper.

Unifix Cubes®, one of the most widely visible classroom manipulatives for elementary school mathematics, are used predominantly in the activities. They provide children with an excellent tool for counting, computing and making patterns. Other manipulatives, such as two-color counters, pattern blocks and attribute logic blocks are also included in the activities. Calculator use is also suggested for certain activities.

By using children's literature and Unifix Cubes® or other appropriate manipulatives, students will be able to:

- ◆ assemble information about mathematical concepts in an understandable way;
- ◆ unfold mathematical concepts beyond the traditional textbook setting;
- ◆ discover mathematical concepts independently;
- ◆ obtain knowledge about mathematics and other subject areas, not generally obtainable in other formats;
- ◆ energize creative thinking, communication and reasoning skills;
- ◆ focus on problem solving strategies and connections to everyday living; and
- ◆ gain an appreciation for literature.

Problem solving, reasoning and proof, communication, connections and representation—all are essential in developing students' understanding of mathematics. As you incorporate the ideas presented in this book into your mathematics instruction, keep in mind that we want to help children become life-long learners, valuing both mathematics and literature.

ALICE IN PASTALAND:
A MATH ADVENTURE

Alexandra Wright

Story Summary

There are lots of pastabilities as Alice falls into a wonderland full of pasta. Alice meets the Math Hatter, the Adder and the Quantum Cat during her adventures. Based on Lewis Carroll's classic tale, children will read and see how Alice is mathematically aware of her surroundings.

Watertown, MA: Charlesbridge Publishing, 1997   ISBN: 1-57091-151-7

Grade Level 2–3

Concepts or Skills

- Sorting
- Classification
- Estimation
- Number sense
- Measurement
- Data analysis
- Patterning

Objectives

- Estimate quantities
- Construct and interpret object or picture graphs
- Use mental math to find sums
- Construct and describe patterns
- Measure objects with standard and nonstandard units

Materials Needed

- Unifix Cubes
- Pasta
- Rulers
- Plastic containers
- Seashells
- Measuring cup or balance scale

Activity 1

Fill a large container with different types or colors of pasta. Have children estimate the number of pieces in the container. Remove the pieces and count them. Next, have children make an object or picture graph showing the types or colors of pasta. Discuss the findings.

Repeat the activity, filling the container with different colors of Unifix Cubes.

Activity 2

Have children measure out one quarter of a cup of pasta or one quarter of a pound of pasta as discussed in the book.

Activity 3

Give each child a ruler and some Unifix Cubes. Discuss how tall Alice was after eating pasta to go through the garden. Have children construct a bar of Unifix Cubes that is approximately 8 inches in length, her height.

Activity 4

Have children draw pictures of things that come in twos, just like the animals did in the story. Let children share their drawings with the class.

Activity 5
Dye some elbow pasta or purchase colored elbow pasta. Have children construct necklaces showing color patterns. Discuss the patterns created.

Activity 6
Fill containers with seashells. Let children estimate how many seashells are in the container. Start with 10, and increase the number in multiples of 10.

Activity 7
Use different sizes and colors of seashells. Have small groups of children sort the shells and describe their sorting criteria.

Give children containers with different types or colors of pasta. Have small groups sort the pasta, and then create different pasta patterns.

Activity 8
In the story, the Queen asks Alice if she likes games. They play a game of musical chairs, singing "She'll Be Coming Round the Pasta When She Comes." Have children do the same, stopping after singing one verse. Just like in the story, take chairs away and continue to play until one child is the winner.

Activity 9
Have children bring favorite family pasta recipes to class. Compile a recipe booklet for families.

Activity 10
Throughout the story, Alice comes across different numbers. For example, Alice is asked to eat 6 letters from the alphabet noodles. Give the children Unifix Cubes and have them make different combinations to show 6.

Writing
Have children pretend they are Alice (or Alex) and write about their own adventures in Pastaland.

Reinforcement
You can evaluate children's estimation and measuring skills by observing the ongoing activities.

You can observe color patterns developed by children and listen to the descriptions of those patterns.

Notes:

AMANDA BEAN'S AMAZING DREAM: A MATHEMATICAL STORY

Cindy Neuschwander

Story Summary

Amanda loves to count. She will count everything that she can. Sometimes, however, she is not fast enough. Amanda's teacher tries to convince her to use multiplication. She has a dream and realizes that, indeed, she can count on multiplication.

New York: Scholastic Press, 1998   ISBN: 0-590-30012-1

Grade Level 2–3

Concepts or Skills
- Beginning multiplication
- Multiples
- Skip counting

Objectives
- Skip count by 2, 5, or 10 to a specified number
- Show basic multiplication as an array

Materials Needed
- Unifix Cubes
- Popcorn kernels

Activity 1
Have children verbally count by ones, twos, fives and tens.

Activity 2
Have children count the number of floor tiles, ceiling tiles, or concrete blocks in the classroom. Discuss other possible ways to determine the total number that might be quicker, such as skip counting.

Activity 3
Use Unifix Cubes to show a simple array for beginning multiplication. For example, 2 x 3 means two rows with three Unifix Cubes in each row. The total number of cubes would be 6, or 3 + 3. Four rows of five cubes would be shown mathematically as 4 x 5, or 5 + 5 + 5 + 5. Although the number of tiles or concrete blocks in a row and the number of rows may be large, students should be able to create an array using Unifix Cubes.

Activity 4
Give a group of children one small bag of popcorn kernels. Have the children decide how they will count the kernels: by ones, twos, fives, or tens.

Activity 5

Prepare small plastic bags filled with Unifix Cubes. Have the children count the number of cubes in each bag using skip counting by a designated number (2, 5, or 10). Then have children write the corresponding multiplication number sentence.

Activity 6

The author suggests reading the book to children first, and then returning to each illustration to talk about how to count the objects on the page. Many great activities are provided at the end of the book for classroom use.

Activity 7

Have children decide on something to count around their homes. Children should count the objects and then explain through pictures and writing how they used multiplication to count the objects.

Writing

Have children respond to prompts, such as the following:

- Multiplication is faster than adding because . . .
- Multiplication plays an important role in our mathematics work because . . .
- Multiplication is like repeated addition because . . .

Reinforcement

Present a particular number of Unifix Cubes to the children. Have them count the cubes using skip counting and then write the corresponding multiplication sentence.

NOTES:

BEEP, BEEP. VROOM, VROOM!

Stuart J. Murphy

Story Summary

Kevin places his toy cars in a particular pattern on a shelf. When his mother calls him to set the table for dinner, his sister Molly plays with the cars. Suddenly, the cars fall from the shelf. Kevin's dad hears the crash of cars. He helps Molly place the cars back on the shelf; however, the pattern is not the same as Kevin's. When he leaves, Molly again plays with the cars and...crash! The cars fall off the shelf. Mom hears the crash and she helps Molly place the cars back on the shelf...in a different pattern. This time, however, the pattern is the same as Kevin's. When he returns to his room, he notices the cars are in the same pattern as when he left. Because Molly is interested in Kevin's cars, her parents bring her an early birthday present...her own cars.

New York: Harper Collins Children's Books, 2000   ISBN: 0-06-446728-7

Grade Level K–1

Concepts or Skills

- Patterning

Objectives

- Recognize, describe and construct patterns

Materials Needed

- Unifix Cubes
- Pasta
- Manila paper

Activity 1

Distribute Unifix Cubes to small groups of children. Have each group sort the cubes by colors. Discuss the idea of groups. Explain to children what a pattern is and demonstrate on the overhead projector with different manipulatives. Have each group make a simple color pattern using the Unifix Cubes and then describe the pattern to the class.

Activity 2

Have children find patterns in the classroom. Discuss the patterns found.

Activity 3

Take children on a pattern walk through the school, pointing out different patterns. Have children describe the patterns they observe.

Activity 4

Give each child a small bag of pasta of different shapes. Have them construct a pattern with the pasta. Then, have them draw and color the pattern on manila paper. Have children orally describe their patterns. Are there similar patterns in the class? Make a pattern book for the library.

Writing

Have children draw or write about topics such as the following:

*   The Patterns I Found at Home
*   The Patterns I Found on the Playground
*   The Patterns I Found on Leaves

Notes:

THE BEST BUG PARADE

Stuart J. Murphy

Story Summary
The story is about a red beetle that asserts he is big—but another bug is bigger and a third is biggest. Now the beetle declares he is small. However, a second bug is smaller and a third is the smallest. As the bugs line up for a bug parade, the beetle states that he is long. A longer caterpillar appears, followed by the longest caterpillar. As expected, the beetle claims that he is now short, only to be proven wrong with the appearance of a shorter bug and then the shortest bug. Finally, all the bugs line up for the best bug parade.

New York: Harper Collins Children's Books, 1996   ISBN: 0-06-446700-7

Grade Level K–2

Concepts or Skills
- Counting
- Ordering by length (long/short), size (large/small), or other attributes

Objectives
- Count to a specified number
- Order a set of objects from shortest to longest
- Order a set of objects from smallest to largest

Materials Needed
- Attribute blocks

Activity 1
As the story is read to the children, have them determine how many bugs are in the parade at each stage. Guide them in making a table or graph to indicate the resulting number.

Activity 2
Have the students draw and color their own bugs. Then have them arrange them according to a designated attribute: size, length, or number of legs.

Activity 3
Go on a field trip in the school yard to collect bugs, or have children and their parents collect a certain number of bugs to place in order by some attribute.

When all the bugs have been collected, have children determine who has the biggest, smallest, longest, or shortest bug.

Activity 4
Using attribute blocks, have children sort according to size (largest/smallest), color, shape, or thickness (thick/thin).

Didax Educational Resources

Activity 5

Have small groups of children line up according to height. Mix groups so that the shortest (tallest) in one group may be the tallest (shortest) in a different group.

Note: The author presents suggestions for several additional activities involving real world objects, cooking, nature and games.

Writing

After the children have ordered various sets, have them make up their own set to order. Have them write their reasoning for their ordering scheme.

Reinforcement

Present a set of three objects to the children to order by some particular attribute. Objects might include circular buttons, balls, pencils, or Cuisenaire Rods.

Additional Resources

Hoban, Tana, *Is It Larger? Is It Smaller?*
Hutchins, Pat, *Titch*
McMillan, Bruce, *Super Super Superwords*

Notes:

BETCHA!

Stuart J. Murphy

Story Summary
Two boys try to estimate the number of jelly beans in a jar in order to win a Planet Toys contest for two tickets to the All-Star Game. Before they estimate the number of jelly beans, the boys estimate quantities and lengths for other real-life situations. The practice helps them win the contest.

New York: Harper Collins Publishers, 1997   ISBN: 0-06-026768-2

Grade Level 1–3

Concepts or Skills
- Estimation of quantity and length

Objectives
- Estimate length with reasonable accuracy
- Measure length with standard and nonstandard units
- Estimate quantity with reasonable accuracy

Materials Needed
- Containers
- Jelly beans
- Unifix Cubes
- Paper clips
- Supermarket ads
- Calculators
- Play money
- String
- Clear plastic cups

Activity 1
Fill a container with jelly beans of one color. Have children estimate the number of jelly beans in the container. List each child's estimate. Have children count the jelly beans, and then discuss class results.

Fill a container with jelly beans of two colors. Repeat the above activity. Discuss whether or not color makes a difference in estimating the total number of jelly beans in the container.

To give children experience in making estimates, count out 10 beans and let them make an estimate. Continue this process, using 20, 30 and 40 beans each time before making a final estimate.

Activity 2
Create an estimating area in the classroom. Each week or every other week, do one of the following types of estimation activities with your children:

- For quantity, containers with: jelly beans, straws, macaroni, spaghetti, seashells, Unifix Cubes, cereal, popcorn kernels
- For length, various lengths of: jump ropes, licorice strings, pencils, string. Give children items such as Unifix Cubes or paper clips to measure the lengths.

Discuss the children's estimates. For various estimation activities, discuss how they might estimate quantity or length.

Activity 3
When estimating quantity, label clear plastic cups with ones, tens and hundreds. After making their estimates, have children count the items, placing them in the ones cup, and making necessary trades to determine the exact number of items.

Activity 4
Encourage children to go with their parents to the grocery store and estimate the amount of money that will be spent. Encourage parents to make an estimate also. Have children compare the estimates.

Activity 5
Collect supermarket ads. Give each child an ad and indicate that he or she has a certain amount of money to spend at the store. Let children estimate the items that they could buy at the store and have them list the items. Were they over, under, or at the actual amount of money? Have children use calculators to determine the actual amount.

Activity 6
Set up a pretend grocery store in the classroom. Have children bring in empty containers of food items and make a display. Give children a pretend shopping list and let them go shopping with play money you distribute. Let them make estimates on what they can purchase. Have them pay for the items, with some children serving as cashiers to make change.

Activity 7
Create estimating teams in the classroom. Let children work in cooperative groups to estimate quantities and lengths. Give each group a special name such as the following and discuss the names: Estimating Team, Calculating Team, Assessing Team, Appraisal Team, Computing Team, Approximating Team, Guessing Team and Ballpark Team.

Writing
After each estimating experience, have children write about how they estimated the quantity or length.

Have children write on such topics as "Why Estimate?" or "Estimating in Our Daily Lives."

> ### Reinforcement
> The activities provide for ongoing assessment as children become more accurate in their estimates.

Notes:

THE BOY WHO STOPPED TIME

Anthony Taber

Story Summary

A young boy named Julian wants to stay up late to watch a special television show. His mother, however, says "No!" Julian watches the pendulum on a clock and decides to stop the pendulum. When he does this, everything around him becomes silent and motionless. He ventures out of the house, only to find that everything has also stopped. After this short trip, he returns home and starts the pendulum swinging.

New York: Margaret K. McElderry Books, 1993   ISBN: 0-689-50460-8

Grade Level 1–3

Concepts or Skills

- Measuring time

Objectives

- Estimate the amount of time to perform certain tasks
- Tell time to the hour, half-hour and quarter-hour
- Compute difference in time

Materials Needed

- Manila paper
- Clock or stopwatch
- Cards numbered 1 through 12
- Cards showing digital times

Activity 1

For each child, write a time on a piece of manila paper (7 a.m., 12 noon, 3:00 p.m., 5:00 p.m., 11:00 p.m.). Distribute the papers and have children draw a picture and write a description of what they would be doing at the indicated time. Discuss the drawings with the class.

Activity 2

Have children estimate how much time it would take to perform certain tasks in the classroom. For example: How many seconds would it take to print your name? How many seconds would it take to complete a particular mathematics assignment? How many seconds would it take to hang up your coat? Time children on the various tasks and compare estimates to the actual times.

Activity 3

Give a number card from 1 to 12 to each of twelve children. Have the children make a circle, forming a clock face. Pair other children, with one child being the hour hand and the other being the minute hand. Give each pair a card with a time shown (3:00, 4:30, etc.) and have them position themselves in the circle to show the given time. Give everyone a chance to be an hour or minute hand.

Activity 4
Have children write story problems involving times. Let them read the problems to the class. Have children solve the problems.

Activity 5
Have children research the history of telling time and clocks.

Writing
Have children write about:
- Why We Need Clocks
- The History of Clocks
- If We Didn't Have Clocks
- The Oldest Clock

Notes:

THE BUTTON BOX

Margarette S. Reid

Story Summary
The story is about a young boy who visits his grandmother. She has a round tin box filled with many different kinds of buttons. The boy likes to sort the buttons into different sets by shape, color, material, number of holes, patterns, thickness and sounds they make. Grandmother and grandson play a game in which they identify attributes of buttons they select.

New York: Penguin Putnam Books for Young Readers, 1990   ISBN: 0-525-44590-0

Grade Level 1–2

Concepts or Skills
- Counting
- Sorting
- Classification
- Estimation
- Ordinal numbers
- Ordering by size

Objectives
- Classify objects by various attributes
- Count to a specified number
- Estimate quantities with reasonable accuracy
- Order objects by size
- Identify ordinal positions up to tenth

Materials Needed
- Containers of buttons for each group of three to four children
- Attribute logic blocks
- Unifix Cubes
- String

Activity 1
Divide the children into small groups of three to four children, with each group having a container filled with buttons. Have children estimate the number of buttons in their container. Then have them count the buttons.

Activity 2
Ask the students to sort the buttons into different sets. Discuss the categories they used: size, shape, number of holes, patterns, material, thickness and so on.

Activity 3
Have each child close his or her eyes, take 5 (10) buttons from the container and order them according to size.

Activity 4
Have each child make a button spinner with string. Listen and discuss the different sounds the spinners make.

Activity 5
Give 10 buttons to each child and ask them to categorize the buttons according to the number of holes they contain: 0, 2, 4, or other.

Activity 6
Arrange 10 buttons in a row. Have children point to a specified ordinal number: first, second, third, up to tenth.

Extensions

Attribute logic blocks provide additional opportunities for sorting by shape, color, size, and thickness. Here are a few suggestions:

1. Find all the large (small) shapes, large squares, small circles.
2. Find all the thick triangles, thin rectangles.
3. Find all the red hexagons, blue circles, yellow triangles.

Unifix Cubes can be used for estimation and color classification. Place several Unifix Cubes in a container and have children estimate how many there are. Have children sort the cubes by color and then make bar graphs showing the frequencies of the various colors.

Writing

Have children write about their favorite type of button.

Have children design and write about a new kind of button.

Reinforcement

Using two or three buttons with holes, have children find the total number of holes.

Using a set of five circular buttons, have children order the buttons according to size.

Using a smaller container filled with buttons, have children estimate how many buttons there are.

Additional Resource

Balka, D. *Attribute Logic Block Activities*. Oak Lawn, IL: Ideal School Supply, 1985. ISBN 0-89099-520-6

Notes:

A CHAIR FOR MY MOTHER

Vera B. Williams

Story Summary

After a fire destroys their home and possessions, Rosa, her mother and her grandmother save money to buy a chair. The tips that Rosa's mother makes as a waitress go into a big jar. Rosa helps at the diner and the boss gives her some money. She puts one-half of this money into the jar. Money that grandmother saves when she buys groceries also goes into the jar. They finally save enough money to buy a beautiful new chair.

New York: Greenwillow Books, 1984   ISBN: 0-688-04074-8

Grade Level 2–3

Concepts or Skills

- Counting coins
- Estimation
- Fractions
- Time

Objectives

- Identify coins and bills
- Count money
- Estimate quantities of money with reasonable accuracy
- Determine one-half of a given amount of money

Materials Needed

- Play money (coins and bills)
- Containers or jars
- Newspaper furniture ads

Activity 1

After reading this story, have children estimate how many pennies are in a large jar. Repeat this estimation activity with smaller jars filled with pennies.

Activity 2

Fill a small jar with a variety of play coins. Again, have the children estimate the amount of money contained in the jar. Then have children sort and count the money. Let them exchange the coins for play bills.

Activity 3

Read the first page of the book: "And every time, I put half of my money in the jar." Give small groups of children bags of coins containing various amounts of money. Have them count the money and determine one-half of the amount.

Activity 4

Fill a container with a fixed amount of play money over a period of several days. Have children make a table or graph showing the amount of money in the container.

Writing

Have children write about an object they would like to buy. They must write about the price of the object and how many days (weeks) it would take to buy the object if they saved a fixed amount of money each day (week).

Notes:

THE CHEERIOS COUNTING BOOK

Barbara Barbieri McGrath

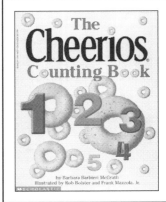

Story Summary

The Cheerios Counting Book helps young readers learn to count using Cheerios cereal, first from 1 to 10, then from 10 to 100.

New York: Scholastic, Inc., 1998   ISBN: 0-590-68357-8

Grade Level K–2

Concepts or Skills
- Counting
- Sorting
- Estimation

Objectives
- Count from 1 to 10
- Count from 10 to 100
- Estimate quantities with reasonable accuracy

Materials Needed
- Cheerios cereal
- Unifix Cubes
- Plastic containers

Activity 1

Give children a container containing Cheerios and have them estimate the number of pieces in the container. Then have them count the number of pieces and record the number.

Fill the same container with Unifix Cubes. First, discuss whether there are the same number of cubes as Cheerios. Again, have children estimate the number of Unifix Cubes in the container and then have them count the cubes.

Activity 2

Give each child a cup of Cheerios and have them make a pattern describing the numbers 1 to 10 as described in the book. Have a child make his or her pattern on the overhead projector using overhead color tiles or two-color counters.

Activity 3

Have children use their Cheerios to make the following groups:
- 2 groups of 5
- 2, 3, 4 (up to 10) groups of 10

As children construct each group, discuss with them the total number of Cheerios in each group. Encourage children to make a pattern for each group.

Activity 4

Give each child several Unifix Cubes. Have them construct a color pattern with the cubes and describe their pattern by drawing pictures or writing in their journal.

Writing

Have children respond to the question "What Did You Learn About Counting with Cheerios?"

Notes:

CUCUMBER SOUP

Vickie Leigh Krudwig

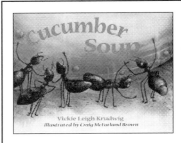

Story Summary

A cucumber falls on an anthill so that there is no way for the ants to enter the hill. Therefore, they enlist the help of many other insects to move the cucumber away from the entrance to their home. Finally, a flea solves the problem and moves the cucumber. Everyone enjoys cucumber soup.

Golden, CO: Fulcrum Publishing, 1998   ISBN: 1-55591-380-6

Grade Level K–2

Concepts or Skills

- Estimation of quantity, weight and length

Objectives

- Estimate quantity with reasonable accuracy
- Estimate weight with reasonable accuracy
- Estimate length with reasonable accuracy
- Measure length with a nonstandard unit

Materials Needed

- Cucumber
- Variety of fruits and vegetables
- Unifix Cubes
- String
- Yarn
- Balance scale

Activity 1

Have children estimate the length of a cucumber displayed in class by cutting pieces of yarn or string. Take children's yarn estimates and measure the cucumber. Have children brainstorm about what other nonstandard units they could use to measure.

Activity 2

Make cucumber soup or dip for the children to taste. The recipe is in the back of the book. Have children bring in recipes that use cucumbers and make a class booklet.

Activity 3

Reread the story and have children use Unifix Cubes as counters to determine the number of insects involved in the story.

Activity 4

Place a cucumber on one side of a balance scale. Have children estimate how many Unifix Cubes would be necessary to balance the scale.

Repeat the activity with other vegetables and fruits.

Didax Educational Resources

Writing

Have children write their own stories entitled "Cucumber Soup" or "Tomato Soup." Have them illustrate their story with their own choice of insects.

Children could also write about "Using a Non-Standard Unit to Measure" or "Why We Need to Know How to Measure."

Notes:

DAVE'S DOWN-TO-EARTH ROCK SHOP

Stuart J. Murphy

Story Summary

Josh is a collector. He collects baseball cards, marbles and buttons with funny sayings on them. When his Uncle Nick sends him a rock from Hawaii, Josh decides to collect rocks. He and his best friend Amy go to Dave's Rock Shop. They see how Dave has organized his rocks by size, shape and other categories. Together, they go rock collecting, organizing their rocks by color. When they take the collection back to Dave, he explains where rocks can be found and how they can tell us about the past. Josh and Amy collect many rocks and divide them into several different categories. Their collection is displayed for all to see.

New York: Harper Collins Children's Books, 2000   ISBN: 0-06-446729-5

Grade Level 1–3

Concepts or Skills

- Classification
- Patterning
- Venn diagrams

Objectives

- Classify objects by various attributes
- Construct and describe a pattern
- Create a Venn diagram for various sets

Materials Needed

- Unifix Cubes
- Attribute blocks
- Beads or buttons
- Containers
- Manila paper
- String

Activity 1

Fill small containers with different colors, sizes and shapes of beads or buttons. Divide the class into small groups and give each group a container of beads. Have them sort the beads by various attributes: color, shape, size. For older children, have them classify by more than one attribute.

Activity 2

In the small groups, have children make various patterns with the beads. Have children explain their patterns to the class or draw their patterns on manila paper.

Repeat this activity using Unifix Cubes.

Activity 3

Give each group some string loops to construct a Venn diagram with two or three loops. Have children classify beads or other objects by two or three attributes.

Didax Educational Resources

Discuss the attributes of the objects in each part of the Venn diagram. Here is an example with two attributes.

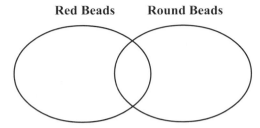

Red Beads   **Round Beads**

Activity 4
Repeat Activity 3 using attribute blocks.

Activity 5
Have children collect and categorize different types of rocks: sedimentary, metamorphic, igneous. Have them describe the rocks: What type? Where found?

Writing
Have children write about :
* Why Do We Need to Classify?
* The Age (or Mathematics) of Rocks
* When I Sort . . .

Notes:

THE DOORBELL RANG

Pat Hutchins

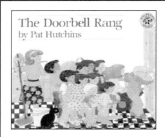

Story Summary

The story is about sharing. Victoria and Sam's mother makes one dozen cookies for them to share. The doorbell rings and friends start coming. Each time it rings, the number of cookies that the children get to share decreases. First, it is six, then three, then two, then one. When the doorbell rang again, no one answers, because everyone will not get a cookie. Finally, Ma answers the door and it is Grandma with lots of cookies to share.

New York: Morrow/Avon, 1989   ISBN: 0-688-09234-9

Grade Level 2–3

Concepts or Skills

- Beginning division
- Multiples
- Skip counting

Objectives

- Skip count by 2, 3, 4, or 6 to a specified number
- Show a basic division fact with markers
- State a basic division fact

Materials Needed

- Cookies, two-color counters, or Unifix Cubes

Activity 1

Begin with two children and 12 cookies. Have the children divide the cookies equally. Start over with four children and 12 cookies. Again, have the children divide the cookies equally. Repeat this activity next with six children and then 12 children. Introduce division notation: $12 \div 2 = 6$, $12 \div 4 = 3$, $12 \div 6 = 2$, $12 \div 12 = 1$.

Activity 2

Use two-color counters or Unifix Cubes as the "cookies." Repeat Activity 1 using the counters or cubes.

Activity 3

Change the number of cookies in the story to 24. Repeat Activity 1. Have children record their results in symbol form: $24 \div 2 = 12$, $24 \div 4 = 6$, $24 \div 6 = 4$, $24 \div 12 = 2$.

Activity 4

Have children practice skip counting by 2, 3, 4, or 6.

Writing
Have children write a story similar to this one, but changing the number of children involved and the number of cookies baked by Ma. Have children describe in their stories how many cookies the children would get each time the doorbell rings.

Notes:

GRANDFATHER TANG'S STORY

Ann Tompert

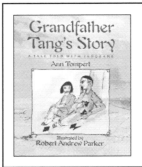

Story Summary
The story is about Grandfather Tang and his granddaughter Little Soo. While playing with tangram puzzles, Grandfather tells Little Soo a story about the fox fairies, Chou and Wu Ling. They could change into various animals, and each would try to outdo the other. When Chou is hurt, Wu Ling comes to his rescue and they chang back to their fox forms.

New York: Crown Publishers, 1990   ISBN: 0-517-57487-X

Grade Level 1–3

Concepts or Skills
- Spatial sense
- Geometric shapes
- Similar triangles
- Area
- Problem solving

Objectives
- Identify the geometric shapes of triangle, square and parallelogram
- Draw the geometric shapes of triangle, square and parallelogram
- Use spatial sense to create or copy geometric shapes

Materials Needed
- Sets of tangrams
- Tangram activity sheets

Activity 1
Distribute sets of tangrams to each child. While reading the story, show children pictures or transparencies of the animals. Distribute copies of the animals on paper and have the children cover the shapes with the set of tangrams. For younger children, show the individual shape outlines. For older children, show just the outline of the animal.

Activity 2
Have children identify the geometric shapes in a set of tangrams: triangle, square, parallelogram. Discuss the attributes of each piece.

Activity 3
Have children create other animals using a set of tangrams. Using a tangram template, copy them onto sheets of paper and distribute to the children to cover.

Activity 4
Larger geometric shapes or other geometric shapes can be constructed with the tangrams. For example, the two small triangles can be oriented to make the medium size triangle or they can be oriented to make the square. Have children make other geometric shapes with the tangrams.

Note
There are numerous books on tangrams available. Most provide an abundance of spatial sense or problem solving activities for children.

Writing

Have children write their own stories involving tangrams. Have them create the sheets corresponding to the objects in their stories.

Notes:

THE GREEDY TRIANGLE

Marilyn Burns

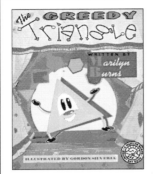

Story Summary
This is a story about a triangle that wants to be another shape because he is tired of doing the same old thing. One day, he goes to the local shapeshifter, who turns the triangle into a quadrilateral. But the triangle is still not happy. He returns to the shapeshifter, who now turns the triangle into a hexagon and then a pentagon. After repeated visits to the shapeshifter, receiving one more side and one more angle, he is changed back to a triangle. He realizes just how important a triangle is in real life.

New York: Scholastic Press, 1994   ISBN: 0-590-48991-7

Grade Level 1–3

Concepts or Skills
- Triangle, square, hexagon, rhombus, parallelogram, pentagon, trapezoid, angle, vertices, edges
- Fractions
- Equivalent fractions

Objectives
- Recognize and name various pentagons
- Identify vertices, edges and angles of polygons
- Recognize and name fractions

Materials Needed
- Pattern blocks
- Manila paper
- Crayons

Activity 1
Take the class on a shape walk and have children point out what shapes they see. Discuss the names of the shapes and their various attributes: edges, vertices, angles. After the walk, have children write about the shapes they saw.

Activity 2
Give each child one pattern block hexagon (yellow). Have them make different combinations of pattern blocks that fit on top of the hexagon. For example, two red trapezoids, six green triangles, and three blue rhombi all fit.

This activity provides an excellent opportunity to begin work with fractions.

The red trapezoid is what part of the hexagon?
The blue rhombus is what part of the hexagon?
The green triangle is what part of the hexagon?
Three green triangles are equivalent to what pattern block?

Activity 3
Give children some pattern blocks and have them write and illustrate a story with the blocks.

Activity 4
Give children a piece of manila paper and have them draw a picture using only triangles.

Writing

Have children write about topics such as the following:

- If I Were a Triangle, I Would . . .
- The Shapes in Our Room (on the Playground, on the Wall)

Reinforcement

Show illustrations of various polygons and have children name the shape, determine the number of vertices and edges, and point out the angles.

Have children point out particular shapes in the room.

△ ☐ ⬠ ⬡ ⬡ ⬡ ⬠ ☐ △ ☐ ⬠ ⬡ ⬡ ⬡ ⬠ ☐ △

Notes:

HARRIET'S HALLOWEEN CANDY

Nancy Carlson

Story Summary

Harriet the dog goes trick-or-treating at Halloween and brings home a big bag of candy, doughnuts and apples. She organizes the candy by colors, sizes and favorites. As she eats her treats, she takes some candy and hides what is left over so that her brother Walt cannot have any. When she eats too much candy, Harriet gets sick. See what happens to the rest of the treats!

New York: Penguin Putnam Books for Young Readers, 1984 ISBN: 0-14-050465-6

Grade Level K–3

Concepts or Skills

- Classification of objects

Objectives

- Sort and classify given objects
- Sort and classify attribute shapes by one or two attributes

Materials Needed

- Attribute blocks (other possibilities include assorted candy, a collection of rocks, or a collection of buttons)

Activity 1

Decide what type of collection the children will sort. Place children into groups of three or four and let them decide how to sort their collection. If attribute blocks are used, children may sort them by shape, color, size, or thickness. Other collections of objects might be sorted by shape, taste, color, size, "favorites," or texture. After each group has sorted its collection of objects, have a member of each group tell other class members how the collection was sorted.

Groups might also move around to another collection of objects and jointly determine how the objects were sorted.

Activity 2

Read *Harriet's Halloween Candy* to the class. Have a jar of Halloween candy for students to look at as you read the book. After finishing, let students estimate the number of pieces in the jar. Then sort the candy by attributes (pick one or two) and count it.

Didax Educational Resources

Extended Activities

Based on each group's classification, have the children make bar graphs to illustrate their collection. Have a member of each group explain the resulting graph.

Give each group of students a bag of "goodies" (teacher's choice) and let the group choose how it would sort and classify the items in the bag.

Writing

Have children write about how they sorted the items.

Reinforcement

The extended activities will provide a great deal of information about how children classify, both in a group setting and individually.

If reinforcement must be done individually and attribute blocks are available, assemble some smaller sets of blocks. Have each child sort the blocks and describe his or her classification scheme.

Prearrange sets of attribute blocks with certain attributes. Have children identify the characteristics of each set.

Notes:

THE HERSHEY'S MILK CHOCOLATE FRACTIONS BOOK

Jerry Pallotta and Rob Bolster

Story Summary

The Hershey's Milk Chocolate Fractions Book illustrates various types of fractions using a whole candy bar as a starting point. Fraction vocabulary is stressed throughout the book. Other fractions, not involving twelfths, are included.

Needham, MA: Title Wave Press, 1999   ISBN: 0-439-13519-2

Grade Level 2–3

Concepts or Skills
- Fractions
- Equivalent fractions
- Lowest terms
- Improper fractions
- Numerator
- Denominator

Objectives
- Recognize equivalent fractions
- Change a fraction to lowest terms
- Recognize improper fractions
- Distinguish between the numerator and denominator of a fraction
- Write the fraction for a given situation

Materials Needed
- Unifix Cubes
- Manila paper
- Crayons
- Hershey's chocolate bars
- Rulers
- Recipes

Activity 1
Give each child a Hershey's chocolate bar and ten Unifix Cubes of one color. First, have them estimate the length of the bar in cubes, and then have them measure it. Discuss their results.

Activity 2
Read the book to the class. Have children carefully unwrap their chocolate bar, placing it on top of the wrapper. The first page shows a whole bar, so let children observe their whole bar and its 12 component pieces. Have children break apart the 12 pieces and stack them. How high is the stack? Measure with Unifix Cubes and with a ruler. Compare results. Continue reading the book and have children show the fractions as described in the book.

Activity 3
Have children bring favorite family recipes that contain chocolate and make a class recipe book, "Our Favorite Chocolate Recipes."

Activity 4
Have children invent a new chocolate bar. They should include the following:
- name of the new bar
- ingredients
- size and/or shape
- design of the wrapper

Have children share their new creation with the class.

Writing
Have children write about topics such as the following:
- My Favorite Candy Bar
- If I Were a Candy Bar, I Would . . .
- Candy Bars and Fractions

Notes:

HOW BIG IS A FOOT?

Rolf Myller

Story Summary

The King wants to give the Queen a very special birthday present. After much thinking, he comes up with the idea of giving her a bed, something that has not been invented. The King calls for his Prime Minister, who calls the carpenter, who calls the apprentice. Since the apprentice doesn't know how big a bed is, the King has the Queen put on her crown and pajamas so he can measure her for the bed. When the bed is complete, it is too small for the Queen. The King had used his foot to measure the perimeter of the bed, and the apprentice had used his foot. They are not the same size! Now, knowing what had happened, the apprentice constructs a bed that fits the Queen perfectly.

New York: Dell Publishing Group, 1991   ISBN: 0-440-40495-9

Grade Level K–3

Concepts or Skills

• Measurement with standard and non standard units

Objectives

• Measure length with standard and nonstandard units
• Describe the differences between measurement with standard units and measurement with nonstandard units

Materials Needed

• Unifix Cubes
• Manila paper
• Piece of wood
• Internet connection
• Scissors
• Rulers

Activity 1

Have children remove their shoes and compare both feet. Are they the same size? Discuss.

Next, have children trace around one of their feet on a piece of manila paper and cut out the foot pattern. Have them measure the following:
• top of their desk
• another child's foot
• how many of their feet from a designated location to the classroom door
• how many feet from the classroom door to a particular location, such as the principal's office, library, playground, or cafeteria

Discuss their findings, comparing various measures. Introduce the idea of a nonstandard unit of measure.

After measuring with nonstandard units and depending on grade level, you may want to give each child a ruler (meter stick, yard stick) to measure some of the items suggested.

Activity 2

Have children work in groups of two, with one child serving as the apprentice and one serving as the "Queen." Have children measure for a bed using their foot outline. Make a class graph showing the number of children for a particular perimeter.

Activity 3
Distribute Unifix Cubes of one color to each child. Have children measure their feet, left and right, in cubes. Make a class graph of foot size. Discuss the graph.

Activity 5
Bring a piece of wood to class. Have groups of children measure the board using various standard and nonstandard units. Discuss their findings. Did each group get the same result?

Writing
Have children write on "Why It Is Important to Know How to Measure in Our Daily Lives."

Reinforcement
The activities provide ongoing assessment of children's abilities to measure with standard or nonstandard units.

Notes:

INCH BY INCH

Leo Lionni

Story Summary
In this classic story, an inchworm convinces a hungry robin that he is useful for measuring the robin's tail. The robin spreads the word to other birds about being measured. However, a nightingale wants his song measured or he will eat the inchworm. While the nightingale sings, the inchworm measures away in the grass until he is far, far away.

New York: Morrow/Avon, 1995   ISBN: 0-688-13283-9

Grade Level 1–3

Concepts or Skills
- Estimating and measuring with standard and nonstandard units
- Graphing

Objectives
- Estimate the length of a line segment with reasonable accuracy
- Measure the length of a line segment using standard and nonstandard units with reasonable accuracy
- Construct a picture or object graph

Materials Needed
- Unifix Cubes
- 2 cm grid paper (page 90)
- Paper clips
- Rulers

Activity 1
Distribute paper clips to children. Have them measure the length and width of their math books, their desktops and the height of their desks.

Activity 2
Distribute Unifix Cubes to children. Have them estimate and then measure the length of their feet in cubes. Have them estimate and then measure their hand spans.

Activity 3
Have children create a class bar graph for foot length, using Unifix Cubes on 2 cm grid paper. Discuss the graph: Who has the longest (shortest) feet? Which foot length occurs most (least)?

Activity 4
Distribute rulers to children. Have them measure their feet with the ruler. Create a class graph of foot length in centimeters or inches. Again, discuss the graph. Are the results any different?

Activity 5
Have children measure five different objects at home. In class, discuss what was measured and the lengths.

Writing

Have children write their own inchworm or centimeter worm story.

Have them write on a topic such as "Why Is Measurement Important?"

Additional Resource

Hightower, Susan A. *Twelve Snails to One Lizard: A Tale of Mischief and Measurement.* New York: Simon & Schuster Books, 1997.

Reinforcement

Select various objects in the classroom and have children measure them using standard and non-standard units.

Notes:

JAMIE O'ROURKE AND THE BIG POTATO

Tomie dePaola

Story Summary

Jamie O'Rourke is lazy and does not want to work. However, his wife, Eileen, knows that the potatoes must be dug up for the winter. She injures herself, and Jamie decides that he needs to visit Father O'Malley. On his way, he meets a leprechaun who helps Jamie solve his problem. In the end, Jamie will not have to work again. The people in the town have agreed to feed him and Eileen if they do not grow any more potatoes.

New York: Penguin Putnam Books for Young Readers, 1997   ISBN: 0-698-11603-8

Grade Level 2–3

Concepts or Skills

- Measuring with nonstandard and standard units
- Estimation of quantity, weight and length
- Graphing

Objectives

- Measure using a nonstandard unit
- Measure using a standard unit
- Estimate weight with reasonable accuracy
- Estimate circumference with reasonable accuracy

Materials Needed

- Baking potatoes
- Other fruits or vegetables
- Balance scale
- String
- Measuring tape
- Girth Record Sheet (page 91)

Activity 1

Make a graph on the board or use the included blackline master on page 92 to make a transparency. Have children write their names in the boxes corresponding to their favorite type of potatoes. Discuss the findings shown on the graph.

Activity 2

Have children estimate the weight of a potato in ounces or grams. Then weigh the potato on a balance scale.

Activity 3

Divide the children into small groups and give each group a potato. Have children measure the "girth" of the potato using string. Have children make a "girth graph" with the pieces of string. Discuss their findings.

Give each group a tape measure and have them determine the girth using the tape measure.

Activity 4

Have on display various fruits and vegetables. Give children pieces of string and have them measure the girth of each. Have individual children use tape measures to measure each of the fruits and vegetables. Have children record their findings on the Girth Record Sheet, and then discuss the results.

Have children estimate the weight of the fruits and vegetables, and then weigh them. Discuss the findings.

Activity 5

Have students bring favorite potato recipes and make a class booklet.

Activity 6

Bring a 10-pound bag of potatoes to class, but do not show the weight label. Have children estimate the weight of the bag. Have children estimate how many potatoes are in the bag.

Writing

Have children write about the findings on their various graphs.

Have children write or draw pictures about topics such as the following:
- Measuring with String or a Measuring Tape
- The Heaviest Fruit (Vegetable)

Have children write their own fruit or vegetable story.

Reinforcement
Have children estimate the weights or circumferences of other objects.

Notes:

JELLY BEANS FOR SALE

Bruce McMillan

Story Summary
The book does not present a story, but merely starts with the price of one jelly bean being 1¢. It provides photographs on the left page showing a one-to-one correspondence between jelly beans and pennies, and then combinations of coins such as 2 nickels and 10 jelly beans or 2 dimes and 5 pennies and 25 jelly beans. The right-hand photograph on each page shows children with jelly beans.

New York: Scholastic Inc., 1996   ISBN: 0-590-86584-6

Grade Level 1–3

Concepts or Skills
- One-to-one correspondence
- Identification of coins (pennies, nickels, dimes, quarters)
- Combinations of coins

Objectives
- Count 1 to 25 pennies
- Identify equivalent amounts of money
- Make equivalent combinations of coins

Materials Needed
- Coins (pennies, nickels, dimes, quarters) or plastic play money
- Jelly beans
- Unifix Cubes

Activity 1
Fill a jar with jelly beans. Have children estimate the number of jelly beans in the jar. Fill the jar with one color (or two colors) of jelly beans. Have children estimate the number of jelly beans in the jar. Ask children questions such as "Does it make a difference what color of jelly beans are in the jar?" Extend the activity by placing Unifix Cubes in a jar. Repeat the estimation activity. Ask questions such as "Will there be more or less Unifix Cubes than jelly beans?"

Activity 2
Fill a jar with pennies. Have children estimate the number of pennies in the jar. After they have given their estimates, tell students the total value of the pennies. Then, ask children what other coins could make an equivalent amount of money. For example, if there are 109 pennies in the jar, then an equivalent amount could be 4 quarters, 1 nickel and 4 pennies. Let students write other combinations.

Activity 3
Walk around the room with a small amount of change in a bag. Have children guess the coins you have in the bag. Provide them with clues such as "I have 8 coins totaling 50¢." One answer could be 6 nickels and 2 dimes. Vary this activity on a regular basis.

Activity 4

As you read this book, use overhead counters and coins to show on a projector the different amounts of money represented in the book.

Activity 5

Give students a small bag of jelly beans and a bag full of coins. Have the children first estimate the number of jelly beans in the bag, record their estimate on paper, and then count the beans. Using the coins, have them make equivalent combinations showing the amount represented. As in Activity 1, extend this, using Unifix Cubes in a bag.

Note

The last pages of the book provide interesting information about the history of jelly beans and their history with former President Reagan.

Writing

Have children write about "If I were a penny, I would . . ."

Have children respond to the question "What other president would you like to see on a coin?"

Reinforcement

Many of the activities provided are self-checking.

Provide children with a small amount of jelly beans (or Unifix Cubes). Have them show various equivalent combinations of coins representing the number of beans.

Provide the children with an amount of change. Have them show the equivalent number of jelly beans or Unifix Cubes.

Notes:

JIM AND THE BEANSTALK

Raymond Briggs

Story Summary

Jim wakes up one morning and finds a plant that is large and rather unusual growing outside his window. He decides to climb the plant and investigate how high it goes. At the top of the plant he finds a castle and a giant. He greets the giant and soon realizes that the giant has some problems. Jim decides to solve those problems.

New York: Penguin Putnam Books for Young Readers, 1997 ISBN: 0-698-11577-5

Grade Level 1–3

Concepts or Skills
- Measurement of length using standard units
- Problems solving
- Estimation

Objectives
- Measure different items using a tape measure or other suitable measurement devices
- Estimate various distances to a reasonable accuracy

Materials Needed
- Unifix Cubes
- Paper clips
- Toothpicks
- Jump rope
- Rulers
- Tape measure

Activity 1
Have children take off their left shoe. Make a shoe graph on the floor by having children line up their shoes according to size. Take off your shoe also and include it in the graph. Label the graph using chalk. Talk about the different shoe sizes and what your shoe size does to the graph. How would the giant's shoe size affect the graph?

Activity 2
Take a jump rope of any size. Have two children hold the jump rope at each end. Let children estimate how long they think the jump rope is. You may want the children to estimate using Unifix Cubes, paper clips, or toothpicks. Measure the length after everyone has estimated. Let the children calculate how far off they were in their estimates. This is a good activity for using a calculator. Who was closest in his or her estimate?

Activity 3
Have children measure different items in their desk, first using a standard unit such as a Unifix Cube and then using a ruler. Items might include books, pencils, pens, or notebooks. Ask the children what differences they noticed when using cubes and when using a ruler.

Didax Educational Resources

Extended Activities

Before class, measure a variety of objects in the classroom with a ruler or other standard units. Tell children the length of the object and let them guess what each object is.

Writing

Have children write about one of the following:

- If Jim did not have a tape measure, how could he solve the giant's problems? What could he use?
- How I Use Measurement in My Daily Life

Reinforcement

Present children with a standard unit of measure such as a cube, paper clip, or a one-centimeter or one-inch segment. Have students use a straightedge to draw line segments of various lengths, and then use the measuring instrument to check their segments.

Notes:

JUST A LITTLE BIT

Ann Tompert

Story Summary

The story involves Elephant and Mouse on a seesaw. The seesaw does not move because of the weight of Elephant is greater than the weight of Mouse. One by one, animals join Mouse on the seesaw to help. Finally, a beetle lands on one of the animals and the seesaw moves.

Boston: Houghton Mifflin Company, 1993   ISBN: 0-395-51527-0

Grade Level 1–3

Concepts or Skills

- Counting
- Basic addition
- Missing addends
- Addition fact strategy of adding 1

Objectives

- Count by ones
- Create simple equations
- Add 1 to a given number
- Find a missing addend in an open number sentence

Materials Needed

- Unifix Cubes or two-color counters for markers
- Math balance scale with hanging weights (or a pan balance)

Activity 1

While reading the story, have children keep track of the number of animals on the seesaw with Mouse. Have children use Unifix Cubes or two-color counters as markers to keep a tally. Older children may record their results on paper.

Activity 2

Use a math balance scale with the children. Label the hanging weights with the names of the animals. If the weights are all the same, place Elephant on one end of the balance and place Mouse closest to the center. Add various animals at points on the scale until it balances. If the weights vary, label the heaviest as Elephant and the lightest as Mouse. Add other animals to the end with Mouse until the scale balances.

Activity 3

Review basic addition facts so that children can understand the idea of an equation: $1 + 2 = 3$, $1 + 5 = 6$, and so on. Discuss how the idea applies to the math balance.

Then let children create various equations using the balance.

Writing

Have the children write their reasons why Mouse and Elephant could not make the seesaw move.

For children in the upper grades, have them do research in books or on the Internet to find average weights of a variety of animals. Using estimation procedures (rounding, front end), have them find combinations of animals that would balance with Elephant. Here are some to start:

Animal	Weight
Mouse	0.79 ounces
African Elephant	7 tons
Ringtail Monkey	6 pounds
Fox	14 pounds
Coyote	75 pounds
Moose	800 pounds
Red Deer	390 pounds
Cow	1800 pounds
Polar Bear	715 pounds
Sheep	150 pounds

Reinforcement

Have children find missing addends for various open number sentences.

Place weights in different positions on each side of the math balance scale. Have students find weights to balance the scale.

Additional Resource

Diagram Group. *Comparisons*. New York: St. Martin's Press, 1980.
ISBN 0-312-15484-4

Notes:

LILLY'S PURPLE PLASTIC PURSE

Kevin Henkes

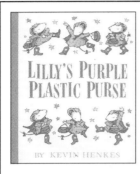

Story Summary

Lilly, a mouse, loves school! She loves all kinds of things about school, such as pencils, chalk, her desk and lunch. She especially likes her teacher, Mr. Slinger. When Lilly goes shopping over the weekend, she buys a brand new purple purse. The purse also plays a catchy tune. She wants to show the purse to the class, but Mr. Slinger says she must do it later. She becomes angry, draws a nasty picture of Mr. Slinger and slips it into his bag. However, Mr. Slinger has already written a very nice note to Lilly about her purse and its contents. Lilly now feels so bad. The next day, she apologizes and Mr. Slinger lets her show her purple purse.

New York: Greenwillow Books, 1996   ISBN: 0-688-12897-1

Grade Level 1–3

Concepts or Skills

- Money

Objectives

- Identify and determine the value of coins
- Determine different combinations of coins that total a designated amount of money

Materials Needed

- Play money
- Purses, wallets, or containers

Activity 1

Have plastic purple purses, wallets, or containers with different combinations of coins totaling 75¢, such as 5 dimes and 5 nickels. Ask children how much money there is.

Continue the activity for a few days with different amounts of money. After repeating the activity, have children create their own problems with a particular amount of money. Let them share their problems with the class.

Activity 2

Present the following problem to the children:

How many different ways can you make change for 25¢?

Have children, working in groups and using play money, construct a table showing the various ways. On page 51 is a table showing the 13 ways.

Vary the amount of money and repeat the activity.

Quarters	Dimes	Nickels	Pennies
1	0	0	0
0	2	1	0
0	2	0	5
0	1	3	0
0	1	2	5
0	1	1	10
0	1	0	15
0	0	5	0
0	0	4	5
0	0	3	10
0	0	2	15
0	0	1	20
0	0	0	25

Writing

Have children write stories about "How Could I Spend 75¢?" or "If I Could Save My Money I Would . . ."

Reinforcement

Have children determine what combinations of coins make up a particular amount of money.

Notes:

LOST AT THE WHITE HOUSE

Lisa Griest

Story Summary
Rena and Rose go to the 1909 White House Easter egg roll. This is Rena's first time going to the annual event. Rena meets President William Howard Taft after a fall. The story is based on Rena's grandmother attending the function in 1909.

Minneapolis, MN: Carolrhoda Books, 1994   ISBN: 0-87614-726-0

Grade Level 1–3

Concepts or Skills
- Estimation of quantity
- Measuring circumference and weight
- Problem solving involving computation

Objectives
- Estimate quantity with reasonable accuracy
- Measure circumferences of objects using a tape measure
- Solve computation problems

Materials Needed
- Container with plastic eggs
- Measuring tapes
- Unifix Cubes
- Balance scale

Activity 1
Have children estimate the number of plastic eggs in a container. Count the eggs and determine whose estimate was closest to the exact number. Repeat the activity with Unifix Cubes in the container.

Activity 2
Have an Easter egg hunt. Write a problem card with an appropriate mathematical problem for each child. Tape the answers on the plastic eggs. Hide the eggs and let each child find his or her answer on an egg.

Activity 3
Have children work in cooperative groups to measure and record the circumference of a plastic egg. Discuss where each group measured. If the eggs are all similar, the circumferences found by all the groups should be reasonably close.

Activity 4
Fill several plastic eggs with a variety of objects, such as rice, cereal, salt, paper clips, thumbtacks, marbles, or sand. Have children weigh each egg on a balance scale. Discuss the different weights obtained. Have children guess what is inside each egg.

Extended Activities

Have children decorate hard-boiled eggs with geometric patterns.

Writing

Let children write about one of the following topics:

- How I Estimated the Number of Eggs in the Container
- Do All Eggs Have the Same Circumference?
- How I Measured the Circumference of an Egg

Notes:

LOTS AND LOTS OF ZEBRA STRIPES

Stephen R. Swinburne

Story Summary
The author of this book explains and shows through colorful pictures how patterns encompass the world. From food or snowflakes to trees or animals, patterns appear. Some are unique, some have a purpose. Patterns can be circles, stripes, or lines. Patterns can be short or go on forever. Patterns can be seasonal.

Honesdale, PA: Boyds Mills Press, 1998   ISBN: 1-56397-707-9

Grade Level 1–3

Concepts or Skills
- Patterning
- Classification

Objectives
- See and describe patterns in our everyday world
- Describe a given number pattern
- Construct a number pattern
- Construct a shape pattern
- Classify objects according to given attributes

Materials Needed
- Unifix Cubes
- Leaves
- Pasta
- Beads
- Buttons
- 0–99 chart (page 93)
- Addition or multiplication chart
- Pattern blocks
- Plastic coins

Activity 1
Ask children to bring different leaves to class. Group children into small groups of three or four. Have the groups classify their leaves by whatever attribute they choose and investigate patterns they observe with the leaves. Discuss the patterns: Did any groups find similar patterns?

Activity 2
In small groups, have children make various patterns with beads, Unifix Cubes, pasta, or buttons. Have children explain their patterns to the class or draw their patterns on manila paper. Before explaining a pattern, let children guess the pattern made by each group.

Activity 3
Take your class on a pattern walk outside. Have them list on paper all the patterns they can see. Share the various patterns observed.

Activity 4
Give each child a 0–99 chart. Have them find and describe various patterns: skip counting by 2, 3, 5, or 10, certain diagonals. Let children color the squares for the numbers described.

Activity 5

Give each child an addition or multiplication chart. Have children find various patterns on the charts. Discuss the patterns. This activity will focus on various fact strategies.

Activity 6

Give some pattern blocks to small groups of children and ask them to construct a repeating pattern. Discuss the patterns.

Using attribute blocks, have children construct patterns involving one, two, or three attributes.

Give each small group several different plastic coins and have them make a pattern using the coins. Have other groups guess the rule for the pattern.

Writing

Have children write about:
- Why Patterns?
- Patterns on the Playground (in the Classroom, at Home)
- My Favorite Number Patterns
- Patterns Make Our World Easier to Live in

Reinforcement

Give children various sets of attribute blocks and have them sort the blocks according to certain attributes.

Show sets of objects that have already been sorted according to certain attributes. Have children determine the attributes used for the sorting.

Show children various number or object patterns and have them find missing entries or the next entry in the pattern.

Notes:

MEASURING PENNY

Loreen Leedy

Story Summary

This is a story of a girl named Lisa who learns to measure with nonstandard and standard units of measure. Her teacher, Mr. Jayson, gives the class a homework assignment that involves measuring different items of each child's choice. Lisa decides to measure her dog, Penny. She measures Penny in a variety of ways: height, length, weight, running times to different destinations. The book will help children learn to measure different items in many ways using everything from standard measuring devices to non-standard devices such as cotton swabs or dog biscuits.

New York: Henry Holt and Company, Inc., 1998   ISBN: 0-8050-5360-3

Grade Level 1–3

Concepts or Skills
- Estimation of quantity
- Measuring length with standard and non-standard units

Objectives
- Estimate and measure length using a non-standard unit of measure
- Estimate and measure length using a standard unit of measure
- Estimate quantities with reasonable accuracy

Materials Needed
- Unifix Cubes
- Paper clips
- Dog biscuits
- Pencils
- Cotton swabs
- Roll of adding machine tape

Activity 1
Have children estimate the number of dog biscuits in a container. Vary the activity by using different sizes of dog biscuits. Discuss whether the size of the biscuits make a difference in estimating.

Activity 2
Give children a homework assignment like Mr. Jayson did in the story. Have children report on their findings.

Activity 3
Divide the class into small groups of 2, 3, or 4 children. Give each group an item to measure, such as the length, width and height of their desk, or the length and width of a piece of paper. Provide various items to use as measuring devices: Unifix Cubes, paper clips, dog biscuits, pencils, cotton swabs, ruler.

Discuss with children the idea of a nonstandard unit of measure and a standard unit of measure. Compare and contrast the results of measuring.

Have children write individually or in their groups about the measuring experience.

Activity 4

Take a roll of adding machine tape, cut off 12-inch strips, and give one to each child. Have them take the strips home and measure the following: parent(s), pet(s), brother(s)/sister(s).

Construct a class graph with their findings. Have children interpret the graph, and then write about their findings.

Activity 5

Have the children make a weekly or Saturday schedule, just like Lisa did for Penny. Let the children discuss their schedules. How are they using their time?

Activity 6

Have children chart the temperature for their city or town for one week. What are differences for consecutive days?

Have children select a city or town shown or listed in the newspaper, television or Internet. Again, have children chart the temperature for one week. Compare and contrast results for various cities. Do temperatures vary in different cities, countries, or continents?

Writing

Have children write about topics such as the following:

- A World Without Clocks
- Measuring in Our Daily Lives

Reinforcement
Provide children with items to measure using nonstandard and standard units.

Notes:

MISS BINDERGARTEN CELEBRATES THE 100TH DAY OF KINDERGARTEN

Joseph Slate

Story Summary
This is a story about Miss Bindergarten and her kindergarten class. They make plans to celebrate the 100th day of school. Each child shows how he or she will celebrate the special day.
New York: Dutton Children's Books, 1998   ISBN: 0-525-46000-4

Grade Level K–1

Concepts or Skills
- Place value
- Number sense
- Number patterns

Objectives
- Show different number patterns up to 100
- Distinguish between even and odd numbers
- Locate numbers on a number line

Materials Needed
- Adding machine tape
- Unifix Cubes
- Stopwatch

Activity 1
Chart each day of school on a calendar, noting the ordinal number names. Discuss whether the day of the month is an even number or an odd number. Have one child per day draw a picture of the day with a number on it. Post the pictures.

Activity 2
Use adding machine tape to make a number line to 100, marking off 2 cm lengths. Have students place Unifix Cubes to make the number line. Make every group of 10 cubes the same color. As the bar of cubes grows, have students count by tens.

Activity 3
Have children bring in 100 items of any snack, such as 100 marshmallows, potato chips, or chocolate chips. Place all the items in a container and give each child a cup of the snacks on the 100th day of class.

Activity 4
Join with the Physical Education teacher to plan activities for the 100th day of class.
- a. 100 lap relay
- b. 100 jumping jacks relay
- c. 100 situps relay
- d. 100 claps

Activity 5

In the classroom, have children sit still at their desks for 100 seconds or stand by their desks for 100 seconds. To begin, tell children that they need to estimate in their minds how long they think 100 seconds is. Start the time. When children think they have reached 100 seconds, they sit (or stand). Keep track of the various times for the students.

Activity 6

For each day, split the date into different parts (20 = 10 + 10 = 19 + 1, etc.). Show groups of 10 using bundles of straws.

Writing

Have children draw pictures with captions to illustrate how the world will change in 100 years.

Have children show the difference between an even number and an odd number.

Reinforcement

Observe the students as they count and break apart numbers.

Notes:

MORE THAN ONE

Miriam Schlein

Story Summary
This is a book that illustrates for children how the number 1 can actually be more than one, depending on what unit is attached to the number. For example, simple 1 include 1 pair, 1 dozen eggs, 1 week, 1 month, 1 year and 1 football team.
New York: Greenwillow Books, 1996   ISBN: 0-688-14102-1

Grade Level 1–2

Concepts or Skills
- Number sense

Objectives
- Discriminate the number one, based on attached units

Materials Needed
- Unifix Cubes
- Empty egg carton
- Pair of shoes
- Wrapping paper
- Calendar
- Student journal

Activity 1
Have children view the following: pair of shoes, empty egg carton, pair of socks, a calendar that shows one week.

Ask children questions such as the following:
- If I have one pair of socks, does this mean I have one or two socks?
- If I have one carton of eggs, does this mean I have one or more than one egg? How many do I have?
- If I point to one week on the calendar, does this mean I have one day? How many days do I have?

Continue this questioning with other items, such as a picture of a sports team. Have children brainstorm to determine their own 1.

Activity 2
Bring in wrapping paper that has many of one object. Ask children how they would count these objects on the paper. Discuss their ideas, and then let them count the objects working in groups.

Activity 3
Have the children make their own counting books and share their books in class.

Activity 4

The book discusses families and how one family can contain two, three, or more people. This idea is illustrated in the book. Group children according the size of family. Have children make a people graph or picture graph, and discuss the resulting graph.

Activity 5

Make bars of 10 Unifix Cubes and distribute one bar to each child. As in Activity 1, discuss the meaning of "1." What about two bars?

Writing

Have children write or draw pictures about topics such as the following:

* What I Know About the Number One
* Some Words Tell Me More

Reinforcement

Have children find other instances where "one is more."

Notes:

ONE HUNDRED HUNGRY ANTS

Elinor J. Pinczes

Story Summary

The story is about 100 hungry ants on their way to a picnic. With the group moving too slowly in single file, the smallest ant suggests a different arrangement to get to the picnic more quickly. Each new arrangement fails to produce more speed. When they finally arrive, the food is all gone.

New York: Houghton Mifflin Company, 1993   ISBN: 0-395-63116-5

Grade Level 2–3

Concepts or Skills

- Counting by ones
- Skip counting
- Beginning multiplication

Objectives

- Count by ones to 100
- Count by tens to 100
- Count by twenties to 100
- Recognize different names for 100: 2 x 50, 4 x 50, 5 x 20

Materials Needed

- Unifix Cubes or two-color counters for markers

Activity 1

While reading the story, have children begin by making a single bar of 100 Unifix Cubes or a row of 100 two-color counters. As the story continues, have children make new arrangements of the cubes as suggested. Discuss whether the new arrangements will, in fact, get the ants to the picnic more quickly.

Activity 2

Divide the class into small groups. Present a new story title, such as "Thirty Hungry Ants." Have each group explore different arrangements of Unifix Cubes or two-color counters that total 30 or the number you have selected.

Activity 3

While children are in small groups, present a story in which the number of ants is a prime number, such as "Seventeen Hungry Ants" or "Twenty-three Hungry Ants." Have the groups explore the possible arrangements of Unifix Cubes or counters. Discuss the class findings.

Activity 4

If multiplication has not yet been introduced, use smaller numbers for the story and begin to introduce basic multiplication facts using Unifix Cubes for the arrays.

Writing

Have children write their own story about hungry ants or other insects, such as bees making honey or crickets making noises.

Notes:

THE PENNY POT

Stuart J. Murphy

Story Summary

Jessie is at the school fair and would like to have her face painted. However, she does not have enough money. At the face painting booth, there is a penny pot where people place their extra pennies. As Jessie's friends get their faces painted, they place pennies in the pot. Eventually, there is enough money for Jessie to get her face painted also.

New York: Harper Collins Publishers, 1998   ISBN: 0-06-027607-X

Grade Level 1–3

Concepts or Skills
- Coin values
- Problem solving

Objectives
- Identify coins
- Determine the value of a given collection of coins
- Construct a table to determine solutions for coin problems

Materials Needed
- Pennies
- Other coins or plastic coins
- Calculators

Activity 1
Give each child one penny. Have them observe both faces and discuss what they see. Make a people graph or object graph for the dates on the pennies. Discuss results of the graph.

Activity 2
Fill a container with pennies. Have children estimate the number of pennies in the container. Count the pennies and discuss how to write the amount in dollars and cents.

Activity 3
Place a certain amount of change in your pocket or hand. For example, tell children that you have 1 quarter, 3 dimes and 4 nickels. Have children use plastic coins or paper cut-outs to determine how much money you have. Continue the activity throughout the school year.

Activity 4
Discuss the different coins: penny, nickel, dime, quarter, half dollar. Tell students that you have a certain number of coins in your hand and ask them how much money you could have. As they respond, write their sums on the board or overhead projector.

Discuss how they might organize all of their responses in a table. What is the smallest or largest amount of money that you could have?

Repeat the activity with a different number of coins.

Activity 5
In the back of the book, Stuart Murphy has devised a game called "Trading Coins." Use the game board and have students play the game.

Activity 6
Have students bring in empty food containers and make a store. Let children go to the store with various amounts of money to buy different items, with other children acting as cashiers.

Activity 7
Take old catalogs and let children do Christmas or birthday shopping for their family using the catalogs. Give each child a set amount of money to spend. Children can use calculators to determine how much is spent. After the activity, discuss who spent the most and least.

Activity 8
The U.S. Mint is now producing new state quarters in the order in which the states were admitted to the Union. Show the new quarters and discuss their obverse faces.

Writing
Have children respond to prompts, such as the following:
- I have five coins: pennies, nickels and dimes. How much money could I have?
- I have five coins: dimes and quarters. How much money could I have?

Reinforcement
The writing assignment mentioned above serves as a good reinforcement tool. Students not only need to find the value of the given number of coins, but also to use problem solving strategies to determine all the possibilities.

Notes:

PEPPER'S JOURNAL

Stuart J. Murphy

Story Summary

This book provides an excellent introduction to journal writing. The story is about Joey, Lisa and a new kitten, Pepper. Lisa keeps a journal documenting Pepper's growth each month until Pepper is one year old. A calendar is provided for each month, along with the events that took place.

New York: Harper Collins Children's Books, 2000   ISBN: 0-06-446723-6

Grade Level 1–3

Concepts or Skills
- Time
- Calendars
- Time lines
- Graphing

Objectives
- Name the months of the year
- Describe a given time line
- Construct a time line
- Construct an object or picture graph

Materials Needed
- String
- Blank cards
- Plastic coins
- Overhead projector
- One-month calendar
- Plastic bags

Activity 1

Introduce the idea of a journal to children. Ask children if they have ever kept a journal. Discuss famous people who have kept daily journals about their lives (presidents and first ladies, scientists, astronauts). Discuss how a journal serves as a time line.

Activity 2

Have children construct their own time line, from birth to the current year. Have them illustrate their time lines by drawing or using actual photographs. Share the time lines in class.

Activity 3

Have children make a one-week calendar. Have them write or illustrate certain events that occurred each day.

Activity 4

For older children, make a one-month calendar and record daily activities. After the month is complete, discuss or have children write about the following:
- How much time did I spend watching TV?
- How much time did I spend reading?
- How much time did I spend doing chores?
- How much time did I spend doing homework?

Didax Educational Resources

Activity 5

In class, have children make a people graph for the month, date, or day when they were born. Have them interpret the graph and write in their journals.

Activity 6

For each day, have children investigate different money combinations. For example, on October 12, we could have 12 pennies, 1 dime and 2 nickels, 12 dollars, or 1 quarter and 2 dimes. Discuss the amounts of money involved.

Using a one-month calendar with small plastic bags for each day, place pennies in the bag corresponding to the date. How much money will we have at the end of the month? For months with 30 days, it will be $4.65; for 31 days, $4.96; for 28 days, $4.06; and for 29 days, $4.35.

Writing

Have children write about:
- The Importance of a Calendar
- The Origin of a Calendar
- My Favorite Month
- Naming a Month

Reinforcement

Provide a time line for some particular event. Have children interpret the time line.

Write the names of the months on cards and have children place them in the correct order.

Notes:

THE PURSE

Kathy Caple

Story Summary

The story is about a girl named Katie. She buys a purse to hold her money, but then realizes she has no money. Katie asks for jobs to do around the house in order to earn some money.

Boston: Houghton Mifflin Company, 1992   ISBN: 0-395-62981-0

Grade Level 2–3

Concepts or Skills

- Money
- Number sense
- Problem solving strategies: tables, lists

Objectives

- Determine combinations of coins for certain amounts of money
- Construct a table showing combinations of coins for certain amounts of money

Materials Needed

- Plastic coins and play bills
- Old wallets and purses
- Grocery ads
- Coupons

Activity 1

Katie has $2.30 to buy a purse. Using play money, have children determine various combinations of coins that total $2.30. Have them discuss how they arrived at their particular combination of coins.

Activity 2

Bring old wallets and purses to class. Price the items and let children determine combinations of bills and coins to buy them.

Activity 3

One of Katie's jobs is to clean her sister's room for 25¢. Have children determine the various combinations of coins that total 25¢. There are 13 combinations. Depending on grade level, have the children organize their results in a table such as the one to the right.

Quarters	Dimes	Nickels	Pennies
1	0	0	0
0	2	1	0
0	2	0	5
0	1	3	0
0	1	2	5
0	1	1	10
0	1	0	15
0	0	5	0
0	0	4	5
0	0	3	10
0	0	2	15
0	0	1	20
0	0	0	25

Didax Educational Resources

Activity 4

Bring grocery store ads from the newspaper. Form cooperative groups and give each group some of the ads. Have them determine what combinations of coins they would use for a particular purchase.

Activity 5

Katie's father gave her 85¢ for clipping coupons. Have children make different combinations that total 85¢.

Activity 6

Take some coins and place them in your pocket or a bag. Walk around the room and shake the coins, just like Katie did with the Band-Aid box. First, have the children estimate how much money is in your pocket. Record their estimates on the board.

Tell them that you have seven coins that total 50¢. Have them determine what coins you have (3 dimes and 4 nickels).

Writing

Have children write about jobs they might do to earn some money. They may also want to write about what they would like to buy with the money they earn.

Reinforcement

Present children with a particular amount of money, such as 45¢ or 52¢. Have children list combinations of coins that will total the given amount.

Individually, have children use plastic coins to show a particular amount.

Notes:

READY, SET, HOP!

Stuart J. Murphy

Story Summary

As they are playing on rocks, the frogs Mattie and Moe decide to have a contest to determine who can hop the most hops and who can hop the farthest in the fewest number of hops. Illustrations in the book show readers how many hops each frog has taken, and then a number sentence is provided. As the contest ends, one of the frog wins, but the other frog needs only one more hop to tie. They are both hot after the competition and decide to jump into the pond—this is one more hop!

New York: Harper Collins Children's Books, 1996   ISBN: 0-06-446702-3

Grade Level 1–3

Concepts or Skills
- Basic addition
- Measurement of length
- Addend
- Equation
- Fact families

Objectives
- Write addition number sentences
- Perform basic addition
- Perform addition with more than two addends
- Measure length with standard and nonstandard units

Materials Needed
- Unifix Cubes
- Number cubes
- Overhead projector
- Meter stick

Activity 1

In groups of two, give children a pair of number cubes. Have one child roll the cubes and the other write and complete a number sentence for the roll. For example, 2 + 3 = 5. Have children reverse their roles and repeat the activity. Also, provide Unifix Cubes for children to model the resulting roll.

For older children, provide three number cubes. Have one roll the cubes and the other write and complete a number sentence with three addends.

Activity 2

Introduce the necessary vocabulary: number sentence, equation, digit, addend, sum. Post the words on the wall.

Activity 3

Distribute Unifix Cubes of two colors to children. Write a number on the board or overhead projector. Have children use the cubes to model an addition number sentence with the cubes. For example, for 12, children might show 5 cubes of one color and 7 cubes of a second color. Record children's results and discuss the number of different ways to show the sum. Discuss special results, such as the commutative property, adding one, and doubles.

Activity 4

Introduce the idea of fact families to relate addition and subtraction. For given numbers in a family, have children write the corresponding fact family members.

For example, with (2, 3, 5): $2 + 3 = 5$, $3 + 2 = 5$, $5 - 3 = 2$ and $5 - 2 = 3$.

Writing

Have children write on topics such as "Mr. and Mrs. Equation" or "The Right Equation."

Notes:

ROMAN NUMERALS I TO MM

Arthur Geisert

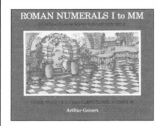

Story Summary

The author uses a pig farm to serve as an "abacus." Readers determine the values of the Roman symbols I, V, X, L, D and M by counting the number of piglets in each picture. Students will also be able to count many different items in the book and learn the various ways the symbols are combined, such as IV, IX and XC.

Boston: Houghton Mifflin Company, 1996   ISBN: 0-395-74519-5

Grade Level 2–3

Concepts or Skills

- Identifying and writing Roman numerals
- Sequencing Roman numerals
- Converting Roman numerals to Hindu-Arabic numerals

Objectives

- Identify and write Roman numerals
- Identify and write Hindu-Arabic numerals
- Count using Roman numerals
- Count using Hindu-Arabic numerals

Materials Needed

- Sets of cards or pieces of paper showing Roman numerals
- Sets of cards or pieces of paper showing Hindu-Arabic numerals
- Picture of a group of pigs

Activity 1

Show students the different symbols for Roman numerals. Discuss the importance of sequencing with Roman numerals.

Activity 2

Have students practice using Roman numerals by writing such things as their ages, addresses, or telephone numbers.

Activity 3

Write different Roman numerals on card stock or paper. Let students translate the numbers into Hindu-Arabic numerals.

Activity 4

Have students count the number of pigs on pages 18 through 22. Have students check their result with the numbers shown on the pages.

Activity 5

Have students count the number of items listed in the book and write the results in Roman numerals.

Writing

Have students write a response to the following question:

Why don't we use Roman numerals all the time in our daily lives?

Notes:

SEA SQUARES

Joy N. Hulme

Story Summary

Various sea creatures are discussed in verse form, starting with one and continuing through ten. For each number of creatures, there is a corresponding number of characteristic features; hence, the name of the book "Sea Squares." For example, there are three fish, each with three stripes; therefore, there are 3 x 3 = 9 stripes.

New York: Hyperion Books for Children, 1993   ISBN: 1-56282-520-8

Grade Level 1–3

Concepts or Skills
- Counting
- Basic addition
- Beginning multiplication
- Square numbers
- Problem solving

Objectives
- Count to 100
- Write addition or multiplication sentences for given information
- Identify and describe square numbers
- Compute sums with two or more addends
- Compute products of the form n x n from 1 x 1 to 10 x 10

Materials Needed
- Unifix Cubes
- 2 cm grid sheet (page 90)

Activity 1

Distribute Unifix Cubes to children. As each page of the book is read, have children form groups of Unifix Cubes to represent the given information. Have them write the corresponding addition number sentences and find the sums (2 + 2 = 4, 3 + 3 + 3 = 9, 4 + 4 + 4 + 4 = 16 and so on).

Activity 2

Distribute Unifix Cubes and 2 cm grid sheets to children. As each page of the book is read, have children form arrays of cubes on the grid sheet. Discuss the shape of each array and discuss the idea of a square.

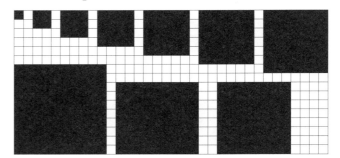

Activity 3

As children create the square arrays, introduce multiplication notation for repeated addition. For example, 3 + 3 + 3 = 3 x 3 or 4 + 4 + 4 + 4 = 4 x 4. Discuss how many rows appear in an array and how many cubes are in each row.

Didax Educational Resources

Writing

Have children write their own "squares" story or "multiplication" story.

Notes:

SEA SUMS

Joy N. Hulme

Story Summary
In verse form much like **Sea Squares**, this book introduces children to a variety of sea creatures. The verses culminate with an illustration of the corresponding number sentences, such as 3 sponges + 4 sponges + 2 sponges = 9 sponges. Certain verses involve only addition, while others involve subtraction or addition and subtraction. The back of the book provides descriptions of the various sea life used in the verses.
New York: Hyperion Books for Children, 1996   ISBN: 0-7868-0170-0

Grade Level K–3

Concepts or Skills
- Counting
- Basic addition
- Basic subtraction
- Addition with more than two addends
- Classification

Objectives
- Classify objects by attributes
- Write addition or subtraction number sentences for given information
- Compute sums with two or more addends
- Compute differences

Materials Needed
- Unifix Cubes
- Manila paper
- Seashells

Activity 1
Distribute seashells to children. Have children classify them by one attribute: size, color, or shape.

Activity 2
Distribute Unifix Cubes of one color to children. As each page of the book is read, have children form groups of cubes corresponding to the verse, combining or taking away the groups according to the particular verse. Have them write the corresponding number sentence.

Activity 3
Have children write and illustrate their own "Sea Sums" book. Read the stories in class and have children use Unifix Cubes to illustrate the number sentences involved in the stories.

Activity 4
Introduce children to Fact Families. For a particular family, discuss the numbers that appear in each member of the family. Give children a set of three numbers for a family and have them write the corresponding number sentences for the family. For example, with (3, 4, 7): $3 + 4 = 7$, $4 + 3 = 7$, $7 - 3 = 4$, $7 - 4 = 3$.

Writing

Have children write about topics such as:

- How are addition and subtraction related?
- What happens when I subtract 1 − 1, or 2 − 2, or 3 − 3?

Notes:

SIX-DINNER SID

Inga Moore

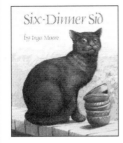

Story Summary

Sid the cat lives on a street where neighbors do not talk to one another. Clever Sid decides to solve this problem by having a meal with each of the six neighbors. None of the neighbors, however, realize that Sid is eating six meals each day. On one particular day, Sid gets a bad cough. Each of the six neighbors takes him to the veterinarian. He has seen six black cats in one day and becomes suspicious. The vet finds the address of the six people and realizes that Sid is, in fact, the same cat.

New York: Simon & Schuster Books for Young Readers, 1993   ISBN: 0-671-79613-5

Grade Level K–2

Concepts or Skills
- Counting
- Skip counting
- Addition
- Multiplication
- Problem solving

Objectives
- Count to a designated number
- Compute sums with single digit addends
- Multiplication sentence to represent repeated addition
- Use a problem solving strategy to solve problems
- Skip count by a designated number

Materials Needed
- Unifix Cubes or counters
- Calculators
- 0 to 99 chart (page 93)

Activity 1

Have children determine how many meals Sid had eaten during the following periods of time: two days, three days, four days, five days, one week, one month. Have children use 6 Unifix Cubes to show the number of meals for each day. Have children share their strategies for finding the total number of meals that Sid ate.

Write the corresponding addition number sentence on the board or overhead. For example, $6 + 6 = 12$, $6 + 6 + 6 = 18$.

For older children, introduce the multiplication sign by showing a short cut way to write the number sentences. For example, $6 + 6 + 6 + 6 = 4 \times 6$.

Activity 2

Have children write and illustrate their own stories involving Sid. Share them in class. For example, Sid had 4 meals each day.

Activity 3

Various beetles have a particular number of spots on their back: 2, 9, 14, 18. Have children write and illustrate stories about beetles. Have them write number sentences for the information presented.

Didax Educational Resources

Activity 4

Have children think about other situations in which repeated addition is present.

- Number of hands, fingers, toes in the class
- Number of tires on tricycles or bicycles
- Number of legs on farm animals
- Number of eggs in certain number of dozens

Activity 5

Give each child a 0 to 99 chart. Have children skip count by a designated number, such as 2, 3, 5, or 10. As they do so, have them place a Unifix Cube on the corresponding multiple. Discuss the various geometric patterns that occur on the chart.

Writing

Writing has been part of the activities above. Also, have children write about:

- Multiplication as Repeated Addition
- Counting by Twos

Reinforcement

Present an array of Unifix Cubes to the children and have them write the corresponding addition or multiplication sentence.

For example, $5 + 5 + 5 = 3 \times 5 = 15$

Notes:

THOSE CALCULATING CROWS!

Alice Wakefield

Story Summary
Farmer Roy's sweet corn has just sprouted when the crows start to appear. Using different plans, Roy tries to scare off the crows, only to find out how crafty the crows can be. Can they count? This book is based on a true story of an experiment by some hunters.

New York: Simon & Schuster Books for Young Readers, 1996   ISBN: 0-698-80483-0

Grade Level K–2

Concepts or Skills
- Counting by ones
- Graphing
- One-to-one correspondence

Objectives
- Count by ones
- Construct a picture or object graph
- Interpret a picture or object graph

Materials Needed
- Unifix Cubes
- Crow cutouts (page 94)

Activity 1
As you read the story to children, show them the illustrations on each page and have them count the number of crows shown. For each crow that is counted, have them take a Unifix Cube. Determine the total number of crows that are shown in the book.

Activity 2
Help children make a graph showing the number of crows on each page. Using the page of crow cutouts, have the children color the illustrations and glue them on their graphs. Then have children interpret the graph. Which page has the most or fewest crows? Are there any pages with the same number of crows?

Activity 3
Repeat Activity 2, but have children use Unifix Cubes to construct their graphs, placing the cubes on 2 cm graph paper.

Activity 4
As people are added to the story scenario, have children write number sentences corresponding to the situations ($1 + 1 = 2$, $2 + 1 = 3$ and so on).

Writing

Here are some "crow" topics for children to write stories about:

- Can Crows Count?
- The Crow that Could Add
- When I Count by Ones

Have children create their own "crow" story.

Notes:

THE VILLAGE OF ROUND AND SQUARE HOUSES

Ann Grifalconi

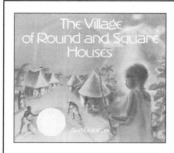

Story Summary
In the remote hills of central Africa in the country of Cameroon is a village called Tos. The women live in round houses and the men live in square houses. A young girl, Osa, listens to her grandmother describe how a volcano eruption caused lava to flow down into the village, burning everything except two houses, one round and one square.

New York: Little, Brown, and Co., 1986   ISBN: 0-316-32862-6

Grade Level 1–3

Concepts or Skills
- Identifying geometric shapes of circle, hexagon, rhombus
- Identifying basic three-dimensional shapes, such as pyramid, cube and rectangular prism
- Describing vertices, faces and edges

Objectives
- Identify, describe and name a variety of geometric shapes
- Identify vertices, edges and faces of three-dimensional shapes

Materials Needed
- Pattern blocks
- Manila paper
- Geofix®

Activity 1
Have children work in cooperative groups of three or four, building houses with pattern blocks. Have each group present its house to the class and describe the shapes that were used to build it.

Activity 2
Have children use manila paper to make round and square furniture for their houses. Discuss the feasibility of this type of furniture.

Activity 3
Have children work in cooperative groups to decide what materials they would need to build a round or square house. Let children bring in materials from home to make their house. After completion of the houses, let each group describe the materials used.

Extended Activities

Show pictures of buildings made in nontraditional shapes, such as round barns, geodesic dome houses, or hexagonal houses. Have children find additional pictures in books or from the Internet.

Using Geofix, build basic pyramids, cubes and prisms. Discuss vertices, edges and faces of each. Have children build houses or structures using Geofix.

Writing

Let children write about one of the following topics:

- Living in a House with No Corners
- My Round House (or My Square House)
- The House I Want to Have When I Grow Up

Have children construct a house using Geofix and write in their journal about the house.

Reinforcement

Present various pattern blocks to individual children and have them name and describe the blocks. The description should include the number of vertices and number of edges.

Have children build a structure from various Geofix, and then have them describe it to you.

Notes:

Book Title	Grade			
	K	1	2	3
Alice in Pastaland: A Math Adventure			√	√
Amanda Bean's Amazing Dream: A Mathematical Story			√	√
Beep, Beep. Vroom, Vroom!	√	√		
The Best Bug Parade	√	√	√	
Betcha!		√	√	√
The Boy Who Stopped Time		√	√	√
The Button Box		√	√	
A Chair for My Mother			√	√
The Cheerios Counting Book	√	√	√	
Cucumber Soup	√	√	√	
Dave's Down-to-Earth Rock Shop		√	√	√
The Doorbell Rang			√	√
Grandfather Tang's Story				
The Greedy Triangle		√	√	√
Harriet's Halloween Candy	√	√	√	√
The Hershey's Milk Chocolate Fractions Book			√	√
How Big is a Foot?	√	√	√	√
Inch by Inch		√	√	√
Jamie O'Rourke and the Big Potato			√	√
Jelly Beans for Sale		√	√	√
Jim and the Beanstalk		√	√	√
Just a Little Bit		√	√	√
Lilly's Purple Plastic Purse		√	√	√
Lost at the White House		√	√	√
Lots and Lots of Zebra Stripes		√	√	√
Measuring Penny		√	√	√
Miss Bindergarten Celebrates the 100th Day of Kindergarten	√	√		
More than One		√	√	

Didax Educational Resources

Book Title	Grade			
	K	1	2	3
One Hundred Hungry Ants			√	√
The Penny Pot		√	√	√
Pepper's Journal		√	√	√
The Purse			√	√
Ready, Set, Hop!		√	√	√
Roman Numerals I to MM			√	√
Sea Squares		√	√	√
Sea Sums	√	√	√	√
Six-Dinner Sid	√	√	√	
Those Calculating Crows!	√	√	√	
The Village of Round and Square Houses		√	√	√

Title	Concept	Addition	Area	Calculators	Calendars	Classification	Counting	Data Analysis	Denominator	Division	Equiv. Fractions	Estimation	Fact Families	Fractions	Graphing	Geometric Shapes	Improper Fractions	Lowest Terms	Measurement	Money	Multiples
Alice in Pastaland						√		√				√							√		
Amanda Bean's Amazing Dream																					√
Beep, Beep. Vroom, Vroom!																					
The Best Bug Parade							√														
Betcha!												√									
The Boy Who Stopped Time																					
The Button Box						√	√					√									
A Chair for My Mother				√								√		√						√	
The Cheerios Counting Book							√					√									
Cucumber Soup												√									
Dave's Down-to-Earth Rock Shop						√															
The Doorbell Rang										√											√
Grandfather Tang's Story			√													√					
The Greedy Triangle											√			√		√					
Harriet's Halloween Candy						√															
The Hershey's Milk Choc. Fraction Book									√		√			√			√	√			
How Big is a Foot?																					
Inch by Inch												√			√				√		
Jamie O'Rourke and the Big Potato												√			√				√		
Jelly Beans for Sale																				√	

Didax Educational Resources

Title	Multiplication	Number Patterns	Number Sense	Numerator	One-to-One Corr.	Ordering	Ordinal Numbers	Patterning	Place Value	Problem Solving	Roman Numerals	Similar Triangles	Skip Counting	Spatial Sense	Square Numbers	Sorting	Subtraction	Time	Timelines	Venn Diagrams
Alice in Pastaland			√					√								√				
Amanda Bean's Amazing Dream	√												√							
Beep, Beep. Vroom, Vroom!								√												
The Best Bug Parade						√														
Betcha!																				
The Boy Who Stopped Time																		√		
The Button Box						√	√									√				
A Chair for My Mother																		√		
The Cheerios Counting Book																√				
Cucumber Soup																				
Dave's Down-to-Earth Rock Shop								√												√
The Doorbell Rang													√							
Grandfather Tang's Story										√		√		√						
The Greedy Triangle																				
Harriet's Halloween Candy																				
The Hershey's Milk Choc. Fraction Book				√																
How Big is a Foot?			√																	
Inch by Inch																				
Jamie O'Rourke and the Big Potato																				
Jelly Beans for Sale					√															

Title	Addition	Area	Calculators	Calendars	Classification	Counting	Data Analysis	Denominator	Division	Equiv. Fractions	Estimation	Fact Families	Fractions	Graphing	Geometric Shapes	Improper Fractions	Lowest Terms	Measurement	Money	Multiples
Jim and the Beanstalk											√							√		
Just a Little Bit	√					√														
Lilly's Purple Plastic Purse																			√	
Lost at the White House											√							√		
Lots and Lots of Zebra Stripes					√															
Measuring Penny											√							√		
Miss Bindergarten . . . Kindergarten																				
More than One																				
One Hundred Hungry Ants						√														
The Penny Pot																			√	
Pepper's Journal				√										√						
The Purse																			√	
Ready, Set, Hop!	√											√						√		
Roman Numerals I to MM																				
Sea Squares	√					√														
Sea Sums	√				√	√														
Six-Dinner Sid	√					√														
Those Calculating Crows						√								√						
Village of Round and Square Houses															√					

Didax Educational Resources

Title	Multiplication	Number Patterns	Number Sense	Numerator	One-to-One Corr.	Ordering	Ordinal Numbers	Patterning	Place Value	Problem Solving	Roman Numerals	Similar Triangles	Skip Counting	Spatial Sense	Square Numbers	Sorting	Subtraction	Time	Timelines	Venn Diagrams
Jim and the Beanstalk										√										
Just a Little Bit																				
Lilly's Purple Plastic Purse																				
Lost at the White House										√										
Lots and Lots of Zebra Stripes								√												
Measuring Penny			√																	
Miss Bindergarten . . . Kindergarten			√						√											
More than One			√																	
One Hundred Hungry Ants	√												√							
The Penny Pot										√										
Pepper's Journal																		√	√	
The Purse			√							√										
Ready, Set, Hop!																				
Roman Numerals I to MM											√									
Sea Squares	√									√										
Sea Sums																				
Six-Dinner Sid	√								√				√							
Those Calculating Crows					√															
Village of Round and Square Houses																				

2 cm Grid Paper

Girth Record Sheet
Jamie O'Rourke and the Big Potato

Item	Estimate	String Measure	Tape Measure

Favorite Potato Graph
Jamie O'Rourke and the Big Potato

Others

Fried Potatoes

Baked Potatoes

Mashed Potatoes

French Fries

TYPE OF POTATO

0-99 Chart

0	1	2	3	4	5	6	7	8	9
10	11	12	13	14	15	16	17	18	19
20	21	22	23	24	25	26	27	28	29
30	31	32	33	34	35	36	37	38	39
40	41	42	43	44	45	46	47	48	49
50	51	52	53	54	55	56	57	58	59
60	61	62	63	64	65	66	67	68	69
70	71	72	73	74	75	76	77	78	79
80	81	82	83	84	85	86	87	88	89
90	91	92	93	94	95	96	97	98	99

Crow Cutouts
Those Calculating Crows!

Subtraction

Sea Sums
by Joy N. Hulme

Tea Out of Bed
by Penny Dale

Splash
by Ann Jonas

Seven Blind Mice *E* *YOU*
by Ed Young

The Empty Pot *E* 398.2 DEM
by Demi Leedy

Elevator Magic *E* 513.2
by Stuart Murphy

A Bag Full of Pups
by Dick Gackenback

Number One, Number Two
by Kay Chorao

Anno's Counting House
by Mitsumasa Anno

Ready, Set, Hop!
by Stuart Murphy

Good Mathematics Reading!

ADDITION

Hunter
by Pat Hutchins

Seven Blind Mice
by Ed Young

So Many Cats
by Beatrice Schenk de Regniers

Popcorn
by Frank Asch

Ten Sly Piranhas
by William Wise

Six-Dinner Sid
by Inga Moore

Anno's Magic Seeds
by Mitsumasa Anno

Domino Addition
by Lynette Long

Sea Sums
by Joy N. Hulme

Mission Addition
by Loreen Leedy

Good Mathematics Reading!

Spatial Sense

Beach Ball—Left, Right
by Bruce McMillan

The Village of Round and Square Houses
by Ann Grifalconi

The Paper Crane
by Molly Bang

Color Zoo
by Lois Ehlert

The Most Wonderful Egg in the World
by Helme Heine

Rosie's Walk
by Pat Hutchins

The Jolly Postman or Other People's Letters
by Janet and Allan Ahlberg

Good Mathematics Reading!

Attributes

The Button Box
by Margarette S. Reid

Fancy Feet
by Patricia Reilly Giff

A Nice Walk in the Jungle
by Nan Bodworth

A String of Beads
by Margarette S. Reid

Big Pumpkin
by Erica Silverman

Tops and Bottoms
by Janet Stevens

Animal, Vegetable or Mineral
by Tana Hoban

Good Mathematics Reading!

Division

A Remainder of One
by Elinor J. Pinczes

The Doorbell Rang
by Pat Hutchins

Artic Fives Arrive
by Elinor J. Pinczes

Good Mathematics
Reading!

Fractions

Gater Pie
by Louise Mathews

Fraction Fun
by David A. Adler

James and the Giant Peach
by Roald Dahl

The Exiles at Home
by Hilary McKay

Here's the Scoop: Follow an Ice-Cream Cone Around the World
by Neale S. Godfrey

Fraction Action
by Loreen Leedy

Eating Fractions
by Bruce McMillan

What's Cooking Jenny Archer?
by Ellen Conford

The Doorbell Rang
by Pat Hutchins

How Many Ways Can You Cut a Pie?
by Jane Belk Moncure

Good Mathematics
Reading!

MONEY

The Money Tree
by Sarah Stewart

The Story of Money
by Betsy Maestro

Count Your Money with Polk Street School
by Patricia Reilly Giff

Pigs Will Be Pigs
by Amy Axelrod

Four Dollars and Fifty Cents
by Eric Kimmel

Ruth's Bake Shop
by Kate Spohn

How the Second Grade got $8,205.50 to Visit the Statue of Liberty
by Nathan Zimelman

Henry's Pennies
by Louise McNamara

The Go-Around Dollar
by Barbara Johnston Adams

We Keep a Story
by Anne Shelby

Good Mathematics
Reading!

Measurement

Sir Circumference and the First Round Table
by Cindy Neuschwander

Thunder Cake
by Patricia Polacco

Titch
by Pat Hutchins

Who Sank the Boat?
by Pamela Allen

Inch by Inch
by Leo Lionni

How Big is a Foot?
by Rolf Myller

Just A Little Bit
by Ann Tompert

The Giant Jam Sandwich
by John Lord Vernon

How Big is a Whale?
by Jinny Johnson

Tiny for a Day
by Dick Gackenback

The Baker's Dozen
by Aaron Shepard

The Magic School Bus Inside the Earth
by Joanna Cole

Good Mathematics
Reading!

Didax Educational Resources